A SPORTS Q&A BOOK

SINCE WHEN IS CATCHING FLIES A SPORT?

Photo credits:

Allsport/Hulton Deutsch—pp. 17, 21, 28
Allsport USA—Rick Stewart: p. 7; Tony Duffy: pp. 8, 13; Todd Warshaw: p. 11; Otto Greule: pp. 12, 16; Ken Levine: p. 14; Brian Bahr: p. 14; David Cannon: pp. 15, 21; Jed Jacobsohn: p. 18; Harry How: p. 19; Jamie Squire: p. 22/end pages; David Leah: p. 22; Chris Cole: p. 22; Nathan Bilow: p. 25; Doug Pensinger: p. 28; other: p. 28
AP/Wide World—Tom Pidgeon: p. 29; other: pp. 9; 13; 23
Archive Photos—Ernest Sisto/New York Times Co.: p. 20; Todd Anderson/Reuters: p. 29; other: pp. 18, 26, 28
FPG International—Jack Zehrt: p. 27; other: p. 18
Icon Sports Media, Inc.—Robert Beck: p. 8; other: pp. 22-23, 25, 26
MBR Images—pp. 3, 7; Jonathan Eric: p. 24
Sporting News/Archive Photos—p. 16

Illustration credits:

Cover and all other illustrations—
Justin Ray Thompson

Visit us at *www.kidsbooks.com.*
Volume discounts available for group purchases.

A SPORTS Q&A BOOK

SINCE WHEN IS CATCHING FLIES A SPORT?

WRITTEN BY
AMY BOWMAN

kidsbooks
Incorporated

Q. Since when is catching flies a sport?

A. Since June 19, 1846, when baseball was born. On that day, baseball as we know it began in Hoboken, New Jersey. This first modern game followed rules set down by an athlete named Alexander Cartwright. In 1842, in New York City, Cartwright founded the first organized baseball club—the Knickerbocker Base Ball Club.

In baseball, a *fly ball*—*fly* for short—is a ball hit up into the air. To score an out, that ball must be caught by a fielder before it touches the ground. A *pop fly* is a ball hit nearly straight up. It usually stays in the infield—the inside of the diamond formed by the four bases on a ball field.

Q. How much does a fly weigh in the boxing ring?

A. Up to 112 pounds—but no more! Flyweight is one of the 17 weight divisions in men's boxing. There is also a junior flyweight division, which has a weight limit of 108 pounds. Boxing's weight divisions range from minimumweight, which is up to 105 pounds, to heavyweight, more than 190 pounds (heaviest).

Q. What kind of trick is a treat for hockey players?

A. A hat trick. A hockey player achieves a hat trick when he or she scores three goals in one game. "The Great One," Wayne Gretzky *(right)*, holds the all-time pro record for hat tricks. He accomplished 50 in his incredible National Hockey League (NHL) career. The term *hat trick* was first used in the 19th century, in the game of cricket. Back then, a cricket player who knocked down three wickets with three consecutive balls was given a new hat. The term stuck, and now athletes in other sports get hat tricks, too. In soccer, as in hockey, a hat trick is when a player scores three times in a single game. A horse-racing hat trick occurs if a jockey or race horse wins three major races in a row. In baseball, the term is sometimes used for the unfortunate feat of striking out three times in one game.

Q. In which sport are players happy to catch a bomb?

A. In football. The *bomb* is a long pass successfully caught, often for a touchdown. It is a good strategy at the beginning of a game to jump ahead. Also, a bomb can bring a win at the end of a game to a team that is behind. So, throwing or catching a bomb can make you a hero, not injure you! Quarterback Dan Marino *(left)*, who retired in 2000 after a 17-year career, threw a record 408 touchdown passes, including a lot of bombs. Jerry Rice, a wide receiver who began his pro career in 1985, has caught the most touchdown passes, including a lot of bombs: 164, as of the end of the 1999-2000 NFL season.

Q. WHICH PRO ATHLETE HAD HIS OWN ARMY?

A. Arnold Palmer *(below)*. "Arnie's Army" is a name first used by sportswriter Johnny Hendrix to describe the mob of fans who cheered for Palmer during the 1958 Masters golf tournament. The fans kept following Palmer, and the name stuck.

Palmer gave his "army" plenty of thrills throughout his career. He won the 1948 Masters tournament and three others. He also won two British Opens and one U.S. Open, among his 60 Professional Golf Association (PGA) Tour titles. In 1980, Palmer entered the World Golf Hall of Fame.

Q. When was Arthur king of the court?

A. In the 1970s. Tennis great Arthur Ashe (above) won the 1970 Australian Open and the 1975 Wimbledon. He made his mark in 1968 by winning the U.S. Amateur Open and U.S. Open. With this achievement, Ashe became the first African American to win a U.S. men's national tennis title. Ashe, who earned 33 singles titles in his 17-year pro career, was elected to the International Tennis Hall of Fame in 1985. The current home of the U.S. Open is named Arthur Ashe Stadium in his honor.

8

Q.
What do tennis players have against love?

A. In tennis, *love* is a score of zero. The term most likely comes from the French word *l'oeuf*, which means "the egg." If you think about the shape of a goose egg, it looks like a zero, and *goose egg* is a slang term used in sports for "no score" or zero. If a tennis player achieves four straight points, he or she gets a *love game*. A *love set* occurs when one opponent wins six games to none. In tennis, *love* always means loss for someone!

Q. Which boxer was king of the jungle in 1974?

A. Muhammad Ali *(standing, right)*. This legend of the ring won the fight he called the "Rumble in the Jungle," held in Kinshasa, Zaire, on October 30, 1974. His opponent was George Foreman, a tough, undefeated fighter, seven years younger than Ali. Foreman was the heavyweight champion at the time, and most people didn't think Ali could beat him. It was in this match that Ali created a boxing strategy called "rope-a-dope." He appeared to take a beating from Foreman in the early rounds, leaning back on the ropes and absorbing punches. But when Foreman began to tire, Ali took over and ultimately knocked him out in the eighth round. Ali was heavyweight champion at three different times in his career—the first boxer to achieve this feat.

A. A *sack* is a type of football tackle. In this tackle, the quarterback is brought down behind the line of scrimmage before he has a chance to pass, run, or hand the ball off to a running back. Quarterbacks hate to get sacked, because they lose yards on the play—and it hurts! Reggie White and Mark Gastineau were great sackers. White has the record for most sacks in a career, 192.5; Gastineau holds the single-season record for sacks, 22 during the 1984 NFL season.

Q. Why do NHL players "light the lamp" when it isn't dark?

A. "Light the lamp" is hockey slang for "score a goal". It refers to the red light on the top of a hockey goal. This light goes on whenever the puck is shot successfully into the goal. It doesn't do much to help the goaltender see, but it confirms that the other team scored! NHL legend Wayne Gretzky has lit the lamp more times than any other player. He holds the record for most career goals—894—and once scored 92 times in a single season! But the record for most goals in a single game has stood since 1920: Joe Malone of Quebec scored *seven* goals in one game that year.

10

A. In 1986. That year, Nancy "Lady Magic" Leiberman-Cline *(left)* became the first woman to play regularly for a men's professional basketball league. She played with "the boys" in the United States Basketball League for two years—one year with the Springfield Fame and one with the Washington Generals. Before that achievement, Leiberman-Cline was the youngest member of the 1976 U.S. women's Olympic basketball team, which won the silver medal. She was a college star for Old Dominion University, leading the team to NCAA championships in 1979 and 1980. One of the biggest forces behind the creation of women's pro ball, Leiberman-Cline played in the first WNBA season with the Phoenix Mercury. She became coach of the Detroit Shock in 1998.

Q. In which sport is a **dummy** smart?

A. Soccer. The *dummy* is a smart move used by an offensive player to get around the other team's defensive players. An offensive player without the ball makes a sudden run toward the goal. The player doing this hopes to draw the defenders' attention away from the teammate who does have the ball. The defenders may think that the runner is moving to receive a pass. If the dummy move works, the player with the ball can pass to a different teammate or try to score a goal.

Q. Which two pro athletes were best at lending a hand?

A. John Stockton *(left)* and Wayne Gretzky. Each holds the all-time record for assists in his sport. To record an assist, a player directly helps another teammate to score a goal. As of the end of the 1999-2000 season, Stockton had earned 13,790 assists in his 16-year NBA career. Gretzky retired from the NHL in 1999 with incredible statistics: Among the 61 hockey records that Gretzky has set or tied, he leads the league in assists with a career total of 1,963. Those are two very helpful people!

Q. Who were the two sweetest boxing champions?

A. "Sugar" Ray Robinson and "Sugar" Ray Leonard. Robinson is known as the "greatest fighter, pound for pound, ever." An incredibly fast fighter, he once threw 31 punches in 25 seconds! In his professional career, from 1940 to 1965, Robinson fought in 202 bouts. He won his first championship—the welterweight—in 1946. Robinson went on to win the middleweight championship in 1951. Over the next decade, he lost it six times and won it five times.

Leonard is the only boxer to win titles in five different weight classes. He did it over a span of 28 pounds (from welterweight to light heavyweight) over nine years (1979 to 1988).

POW!

SUGAR

SUGAR

Q. Who was a perfect little girl at the 1976 Olympics?

A. Nadia Comaneci (*above*). Comaneci was just 14 years old at the 1976 games in Montreal, but she made Olympic history. This Romanian gymnast earned a score of ten in two events: the uneven parallel bars and the balance beam. It was the first time ever that the judges had handed out a perfect score, and they gave Comaneci two! In that Olympics, she earned three gold medals, one silver medal for her team's finish, and one bronze medal for floor exercise. Comaneci's outstanding performance brought lots of attention to the sport of gymnastics, which continues today.

Q. Who played a Broadway role at Super Bowl III?

A. Quarterback Joe Namath (*above*), nicknamed "Broadway Joe" for his flashy, confident, man-about-town style. In 1968, Namath led his team, the New York Jets, to the American Football League (AFL) championship. They were set to play the Baltimore Colts in the pro football championship game, now known as Super Bowl III. Everyone thought that the Colts would win easily. But the week before the game, Namath made a guarantee to the press that the Jets would win! Incredibly, his boast came true with a 16-to-7 Jets win, one of the biggest upsets in Super Bowl history.

Q. Why would a baseball pitcher THROW CHEESE?

A. To overpower a batter. *Cheese* is a slang word used in baseball for the fastball. Dennis Eckersley *(left)*, a great pitcher from 1975 to 1998, once called himself the "Cheese Master" because of his ability to throw fastballs past batters. In the 19th century, the term *cheese* was used for anything first-rate in quality. The expression "that's the cheese" comes from this meaning. A fastball is often a player's best pitch—the one he uses to keep a batter from getting a hit. If the fastball is good enough, all the batter can do is smell it (like stinky cheese) as it goes by.

Q. When does the tennis field get seeded?

A. Before a tournament—but you won't see plants sprout from *these* seeds. In tennis, seeding is the calculated placement of the highest-ranked athletes in the tournament schedule. It is done so that the best players will not meet in the early rounds of the tournament and eliminate each other. Seeding began at Wimbledon in the 1920s. Sixteen is now the standard number of seeds at major tournaments. The players considered most likely to win are ranked from one to sixteen. If the competition runs according to seeding, the athletes ranked one and two will play each other in the final match.

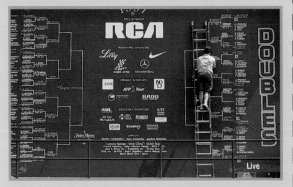

Q.
What does a golfer do when he is caught in an impossible lie?

A. He can move his ball two club lengths and take another shot. He also has to take a one-stroke penalty. For a golfer, *lie* is the type of ground his ball sits on. If he takes a shot and his ball lands where it cannot be moved forward—in a tree or against a wall, for example—he is faced with an *impossible lie*. A golf game is scored by the number of strokes, or shots, a player takes to sink his or her ball in each hole. (The lower the number, the better.) So a good lie helps your score a lot more than a bad one!

Q. WHY DON'T PENALTY KILLERS GET ARRESTED?

A. Because they aren't criminals, they are members of a hockey team. When a player breaks certain rules during a hockey game, he is sent to the penalty box. During the time this player must sit out of the game—usually about two minutes—his team is on the ice with one fewer player than the opponents. The opponents, who try to take advantage of this, are said to be on a *power play*. They bring in their best offensive athletes to shoot for a goal. To prevent the goal, the other team calls on its best defensive players— the penalty killers!

15

Q. Why was dunking against the law in 1968?

A. Because Kareem Abdul-Jabbar was really good at it. Abdul-Jabbar (above), then known as Lew Alcindor, played basketball for UCLA in the late 1960s. He so dominated the game with his skill and height that the NCAA outlawed dunking the basketball, thinking that it would make Abdul-Jabbar less of a threat. It didn't. He won three NCAA championships with UCLA and was named Most Valuable Player (MVP) three years in a row (1967 through 1969). Eventually, in 1977, the dunk was allowed back in college basketball. As for Abdul-Jabbar, he went on to win six NBA championships—one with the Milwaukee Bucks and five with the Los Angeles Lakers. He holds the all-time pro records for most games played—1,560—and most goals scored—15,837.

Q. Which two pro players are best known for theft?

A. Rickey Henderson (below) and John Stockton. Each holds the all-time record for steals in his sport. Through the 1999-2000 season, Stockton—an NBA guard—had stolen the ball 2,844 times in 1,258 games. He had been named to the NBA's All-Defensive Team three times and was a member of two Olympic Dream Teams. Henderson puts his talent to use in major-league baseball. By the end of the 2000 season—his 22nd in pro baseball—he had stolen 1,370 bases and scored 2,178 runs! Those numbers put him fifth on the all-time list.

Q. Where do Olympic birdies fly fastest?

A. On a badminton court! Believe it or not, badminton is one of the world's fastest racquet sports. In competition, the shuttlecock, or birdie, can fly at speeds close to 200 miles per hour. Just like in the backyard game, Olympic badminton players hit the birdie over a net with a light-weight racket. They need to have quick reflexes and agility. Badminton was first played at the Summer Olympics in 1972 as a demonstration sport and became a full medal sport in 1992. It has been popular in England since the 1870s.

Q. Why did winning just two Olympic medals make Jim Thorpe "the greatest athlete in the world"?

A. He won gold in both the pentathlon and the decathlon—a total of 15 events! To win these two competitions in 1912, Thorpe *(above)* had to master 15 diverse categories of athletics, from pistol shooting to swimming. The Summer Olympics were held in Stockholm that year. When King Gustav V of Sweden presented Thorpe with the medals, he remarked, "You sir, are the greatest athlete in the world." It is reported that Thorpe replied, "Thanks, King!" After the Olympics, Thorpe played both professional baseball and football to great success. In 1950, a poll of Associated Press sportswriters voted him the greatest athlete of the first half of the 20th century.

Q. When baseball fans yell for "Big Mac," do they want a burger?

A. Maybe, but it's more likely that they are cheering for Mark "Big Mac" McGwire *(right)* of the St. Louis Cardinals. In 1998, he broke the long-standing single-season home-run record of 61—and passed that number again in 1999. The 61-homer record was set in 1961 by New York Yankee Roger Maris *(below)*, who bypassed the 60-homer record set by another Yankee, Babe Ruth, in 1927. Maris's record had seemed untouchable until Big Mac used his big bat to smash 70 homers—the new record—in 1998. Throughout the 1998 season, Sammy Sosa of the Chicago Cubs raced Big Mac for the record. "Slammin' Sammy" finished the season with 66 home runs.

Q. How does a tennis player hit a grand slam?

A. Not with a baseball bat! He or she wins the Australian Open, French Open, Wimbledon, and U.S. Open tournaments. The first tennis player to achieve this feat was Don Budge *(below)*, in 1938. The term *grand slam* is most often used to describe a home run when the bases are loaded in baseball, but it also is used for an outstanding achievement in other sports. For example, a pro golfer can get a grand slam by winning the British Open, U.S. Open, PGA Championship, and Masters golf tournaments.

Q. In which **NFL** championship game should the players have worn skates?

A. The "Ice Bowl" of 1967. The Green Bay Packers and the Dallas Cowboys played this game on December 31, 1967, on "the frozen tundra of Lambeau Field." The temperature at game time was 13 degrees below zero (Fahrenheit). A new heating system had been set up in the field. It was supposed to keep the top few inches of ground from freezing during the game, but the ground froze solid as soon as the field was uncovered! The Packers slid their way to a victory of 21-17 over the Cowboys.

Q. What do you get when you cross a skateboarder with a surfer?

A. A snowboarder! The idea of snowboarding began in 1965, when Sherman Poppen strapped skis together to make a winter surfboard, called a Snurfer. Modern snowboarding, which took off in the 1980s and 1990s, uses moves from both skateboarding and surfing. It became an Olympic sport at the 1998 winter games in Nagano, Japan. The two events were the half-pipe and the giant slalom. In the half-pipe, athletes ride up to the edge of a U-shaped course, leap off, and perform tricks in the air. The giant slalom is a course of gates down a slope. The fastest snowboarder who doesn't miss a gate wins.

Q. When did the big dipper scoop the biggest score in the NBA?

Q. What might a baseball player do with a *frozen rope*?

A. Get to first base. *Frozen rope* is a slang term for a hard-hit line drive. The path that the ball takes in a line drive is straight and low—like a rope being stretched out into the field. You might also hear this type of hit called a *clothesline*. When the ball is hit really hard, its path appears rigid, or *frozen*. A line drive is much more difficult to catch than a fly ball. The fly ball's path up into the air gives the fielder more time to judge where it will come down and to get in position to catch it. The swiftness of a line drive allows little time for a fielder to react, and the batter has a better chance of reaching base safely.

A. March 2, 1962, when Wilt "the Big Dipper" Chamberlain scored an incredible 100 points against the New York Knicks. This feat has not been matched by any other pro basketball player. In 1960, Chamberlain (*above, far left*) became the first NBA athlete to be named both Rookie of the Year and Most Valuable Player. He averaged 27 rebounds and 37.6 points per game that year! He scored a whopping 31,419 points during his 14-year career, and is at or near the top of many NBA record lists. Also known as "Wilt the Stilt," he is considered one of the greatest offensive players of all time.

Q. How would the Golden Bear

get out of a trap?

A. If it were a sand trap, he probably would use a club with a flat edge, called a wedge. Jack "The Golden Bear" Nicklaus *(above)* has spent a lot of time on golf courses, avoiding sand traps and other hazards, which can keep you from advancing your ball. He has been very successful at it: Nicklaus holds records for most PGA major tournament wins (20) and most titles overall (70). He was named Golfer of the Century by the PGA in 1988.

Q. Whose "rocky" boxing career never hit a bump?

A. Rocky Marciano's. He is the only professional boxing champion to retire with a perfect record. At the end of Marciano's impressive career, he had 49 wins and no losses. Out of those 49 victories, he won 43 of them by knockout! Marciano *(below, at left)* gained the heavyweight championship title in September 1952—and then defended it six times. He stopped boxing in 1955 at the age of 32. In 1990, Marciano was inducted into the International Boxing Hall of Fame.

Q. HOW DO YOU MAKE A BICYCLE KICK?

A. You jump up in the air and pedal your legs! The bicycle kick—also known as a scissor kick—is a soccer technique. It is very difficult to perform, and thrilling to watch. In making this kick, a player must turn his body as if he is going to do a backward flip. Then he kicks the ball with his legs above his head! The first athlete to perform the bicycle kick regularly was a Brazilian named Leonidas. He played soccer in the 1930s and was known as the "Black Diamond" and the "Rubber Man." Leonidas was so good at the bicycle kick that he could control the ball with one foot and kick it with the other.

Q. Do dimples just make a golf ball look cuter?

A. No, those little dents also help it move better. The first golf balls made with dimples came into use in 1880. Before that time, golfers had noticed that their balls flew better after they had been hit a while. Being scuffed actually made the ball more effective! This idea eventually led to a ball produced with a dimple pattern. Today, all golf balls have dimples. Also, golf balls must be at least 1.68 inches in diameter and weigh no more than 1.620 ounces.

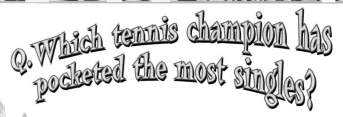

Q. Which tennis champion has pocketed the most singles?

A. Martina Navratilova. She has more pro tennis singles titles than any other player, male or female, with 167 tournament wins. Navratilova has also earned more than $20 million! Among her victories are a record nine Wimbledon titles, three Australian Opens, two French Opens, and four U.S. Opens. In addition to her singles successes, Navratilova paired with Pam Shriver to form the best women's doubles team of all time. Over Navratilova's stellar 21-year career, she was ranked the number-one player in the world seven times.

Q. How wide is an NHL player's goalmouth?

A.
Six feet! A goalmouth isn't found on a hockey player's face. It's the open space of a hockey goal, which is six feet wide by four feet tall. The player who defends this area is called a goaltender, or goalie. NHL goalie Terry Sawchuk *(right)* has been the best at this job so far. He played 971 games in his 21-year career and won 447 games. Out of those wins, Sawchuk recorded 103 shutouts— games in which the opposing team was unable to score any goals. NHL player Ron Hextall was impressive, too. On December 8, 1987, he became the first goalie to score a goal in the opposing team's net!

23

Q. WHEN DO BASKETBALL PLAYERS USE THE BACK DOOR?

A. When they want to get around the opposing team. The *back door* is a basketball strategy used against a very aggressive defensive player. In this play, the person who is going to receive a pass positions herself on an outside wing of the court. Then she moves as if going toward the teammate who has the ball. When the defender tries to block the throw by moving between the receiver and the passer, the receiver quickly reverses direction. She moves back toward the hoop, receives the pass, then takes an easy shot at the basket.

Q. Where can you see a tiger shoot eagles?

A. On any golf course where Eldrick "Tiger" Woods *(left)* is competing. In 1994, at age 18, Woods became the youngest golfer and first nonwhite golfer to win the U.S. Amateur tournament. He won it again in 1995 and in 1996. After turning pro, Woods won three major tournaments—the 1997 Masters, the 1999 PGA Championship, and the 2000 U.S. Open—and is still going strong.

Like any golfer, Woods must enjoy shooting eagles. An *eagle* is a score of two under par. *Par* is the number of strokes that it should take a golfer to get his or her ball in the hole. Each hole is assigned par based on its difficulty. If you sink your ball in one stroke less than par, you've shot a *birdie*!

Q. In which Olympic sport can you watch a Flying Dutchman?

A. In yachting. There are 10 different divisions of Olympic yachting events, and the Flying Dutchman is one of them. In the Flying Dutchman, just two crew members sail a boat that is 19 feet, 10 inches long. The most unusual thing about this event is that one crew member uses a trapeze to help balance and steer the boat! The trapeze is attached to a rope that ties him to the craft and lets him lean outside of it. At times, he is leaning so far out of the boat that he is horizontal to the water! This makes the event very exciting to watch.

Q. Who used his head and his feet to achieve his career goals?

A. Pelé, a soccer superstar from Brazil. (His real name is Edson Arantes do Nascimento.) This legendary athlete used his fleet feet to score 1,281 goals in his 22–year professional career. Pelé *(right)* played in his first World Cup championship in 1958, when he was only 17 years old. He made two goals in that game!

Pelé is the only athlete to have been a member of three World Cup championship teams. He played for the winning Brazilian team in 1958, 1962, and 1970. Pelé came to the United States in 1975 and played with the New York Cosmos in the North American Soccer League (NASL). His presence in this league brought respect-ability to pro soccer in the U.S. In 1998, Pelé was chosen for the World Team of the Twentieth Century.

Q. Who played ball on the ground, but was known for his game in the air?

A. Michael Jordan *(below)*. Jordan retired from playing professional basketball in January 1999, but his action on the court will be remembered for a long time. When Jordan jumped, he could stay so long and move so well in the air that he seemed to be flying. He appeared to float while he threw a pass or shot a basket over the heads of his opponents. Jordan's breathtaking style of play earned him the nickname "Air." Jordan is the only athlete, in any sport, to win six Most Valuable Player titles and to play on six championship teams.

Q. Which boxing star stayed up for more than 11 years?

A. Joe Louis. He may have been knocked down a few times, but "The Brown Bomber" held the heavyweight boxing title longer than anyone: 11 years and 252 days. This may be a record for all boxing weight divisions. Louis *(below)* began his reign on June 22, 1937. He defended his title a record 25 times before hanging up his gloves on March 1, 1949. Louis came out of retirement in 1950 and tried to win back the heavyweight championship, but failed twice. Louis finished with a career record of 63 wins and 3 losses (including 49 knockouts).

Q. Who rushed to get into the Pro Football Hall of Fame?

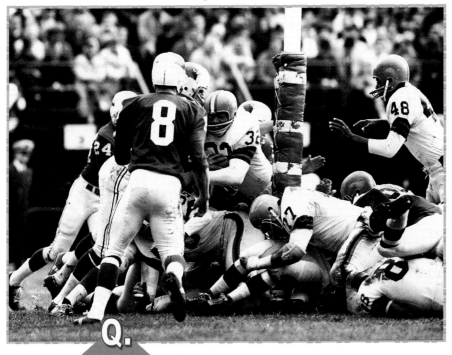

A. Jim Brown *(#32 at left)*. He made a career of gaining ground. Perhaps the greatest running back ever, he led the National Football League (NFL) in rushing—gaining yards—eight out of his nine years in pro football. In his first year, 1957, he was named Rookie of the Year *and* Most Valuable Player. He is the only player among the top ten all-time running backs to have averaged more than five rushing yards per carry. His career total is 12,312 yards! Brown was elected to the Hall of Fame in 1971.

Q. Which country has the greatest kicks?

A. Brazil. It is the only country to have appeared in every World Cup soccer tournament. This international tournament has been held every four years since 1930, except in 1942 and 1946 (during and just after World War II). More than 100 countries now participate. The Brazilian team has won the championship a record-setting four times! In fact, Brazil owns the original World Cup—called the Jules Rimet Trophy—which was retired in 1970 after they won it for the third time. Soccer greats Leonidas, Pelé, and Ronaldo are all from Brazil.

POW!

Q. When did an Iron Man pass the Iron Horse?

A. On September 6, 1995. That day, "Iron Man" Cal Ripken Jr. *(below)* played in his 2,131st major-league baseball game in a row (and hit a home run, too)! With that game, Ripken broke the long-standing record of 2,130 consecutive games held by Lou "The Iron Horse" Gehrig. Gehrig *(above)* set his record on April 30, 1939, beating the 16-year-old record of Everett Scott by 823 games.

Of Gehrig's records that still stand, one is his grand-slam home-run total: He is number one on the all-time grand-slams list, with 23. (In baseball, a *grand slam* is a homer hit with the bases loaded.) Gehrig was inducted into the National Baseball Hall of Fame in 1939. As for Ripken, he kept going after breaking Gehrig's consecutive-game streak. Ripken's streak ended at 2,632 consecutive games on September 20, 1998, when he finally sat out a game. It is unlikely that anyone will ever pass him.

Q. Which two pro athletes were just "babes" when they achieved fame?

A. George Herman Ruth *(right)* and Mildred Didrikson Zaharias *(above)*. They weren't newborns when they played, but both were called "Babe." Babe Ruth was baseball's home-run king in the 1920s and 1930s and still ranks second in all-time total home runs, with 714. You will find his name on nearly every other batting record list, as well. This great athlete not only hit and played the outfield, but began his career as a pitching star!

When Zaharias was a child, she played baseball so well that people started calling her "Babe," after Ruth. She went on to excel in other sports, winning two gold medals and one silver medal in track and field at the 1932 Olympics. Babe Didrikson Zaharias is best known, however, for her career in golf. She won her first championship in 1935 and won three U.S. Opens (in 1948, 1950, and 1954), among her many victories. In 1949, she helped found the Ladies' Professional Golf Association.

Q. Who was the "baby" at the first women's World Cup Soccer final?

A. Mia Hamm *(left)* in 1999. At 19 years old, she was the youngest member of the U.S. Women's National Team. They competed in, and won, the first women's World Cup final, against Norway. Hamm made the team when she was just 15, becoming the youngest player ever to join. In her already amazing career, Hamm has been a member of the 1996 U.S. women's Olympic soccer team, which won a gold medal, and the 1999 U.S. World Cup championship team. Hamm's 108th goal, in May 1999, made her the all-time scoring leader in international soccer (men's and women's). She has scored many more since then!

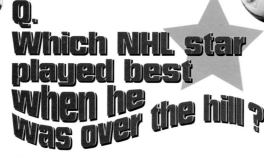

Q. Which NHL star played best when he was over the hill?

A. Gordie Howe *(right).* "Mr. Hockey" had his greatest season in 1968-1969, when he was 40 years old! He scored more than 100 points that season—44 goals and 59 assists—for the only time in his career. Howe just kept playing. He appeared in a total of 23 NHL All-Star games. In his last one, he was 51 years old. Howe glided through a record 32 seasons before hanging up his skates.

Glossary

Agility: The ability to move with flexibility and ease.

Decathalon: An Olympic competition comprised of 10 track-and-field events.

Defense: The act of guarding a team's goal area.

Goaltender: The person who defends the goal area. The goaltender is often called the goalie.

Line of scrimmage: The line where each football play starts.

Offense: The act of trying to score.

Penalty: Punishment given to a player or team for breaking a rule of the game.

Pentathalon: An Olympic competition comprised of five events.

Running back: A speedy football player to whom the quarterback often throws the ball.

Sand trap: A sand-filled dip in the ground on a golf course, designed to be difficult for a golfer to hit his or her ball out. Sand traps are sometimes called bunkers.

Shuttlecock: The rubber-tipped, cone-shaped object hit over the net in badminton. Shuttlecocks are also known as birdies.

Slalom: Skiing or snowboarding in a zigzag course between obstacles, usually flags.

Touchdown: The act of scoring six points in football by carrying the ball into the opposing team's end zone, or goal.